YOU MAKE **IT** WORK

RADIO

Authors: George and Shirley Coulter

Rourke Publications, Inc.
Vero Beach, Florida 32964

About the Authors

Award-winning teachers in the state of Wisconsin,
George and Shirley Coulter have now retired, but
remain active in the field of science education,
designing and presenting teacher workshops. Both
are published authors of books and articles in
national, professional journals in the field of science
education.

A book by Market Square Communications Incorporated
Pamela J.P. Schroeder, Editor
Sandra J. Shekels, Illustrator

Photo Credits
Page 23 "I Love A Mystery" photo © courtesy of Westwood One Incorporated; page 24 photo ©
Wisconsin Department of Natural Resources.

Acknowledgements
Thanks to the Stevens Point Fire Department and WIZD radio, Plover, WI, for their assistance in
arranging photo locations.

Library of Congress Cataloging-in-Publication Data

Coulter, George, 1934-
    Radio / authors, George and Shirley Coulter.
       p. cm. — (You make it work)
    Includes index.
    Summary: Explains how radio works, discussing the different kinds of
air waves, how a radio signal gets into your radio, and how remote control
signals, beepers, CBs, and walkie-talkies work.
    ISBN 0-86625-584-2
    1. Radio—Juvenile literature. [1. Radio.] I. Coulter, Shirley,
1936-   . II. Title. III. Series.
TK6550.7.C64 1996
621.384—dc20   96-3906
                                   CIP
                                   AC

Printed in the U.S.A.

Illustrations are simplified examples meant to show general concepts rather than specific
technical detail.

TABLE OF CONTENTS

CHAPTER ONE

TUNE IN TO RADIO

It's 6 a.m. Click! Your radio alarm blares into life and welcomes you to a new day. As you walk in for breakfast, your dad spins the tuning knob on the kitchen radio. He's looking for the local news. Will there be school after that storm last night? You bet.

Your mom pops some oatmeal into the microwave. Suddenly, her beeper goes off. She calls work on your cordless phone to find out what's up. You flip on the TV to catch a morning show before school.

A radio, a microwave, a TV—are these things that you use? Have you ever plugged your headphones into a portable radio, or flown on an airplane? All these things depend on **radio waves** (RAY dee oh WAYVZ) to work.

Invisible radio waves are everywhere around you—all the time.

They bring the signals your TV needs to make pictures and sound. They heat up the food in your microwave, and make beepers beep. Radar that uses radio waves at the airport helps air controllers direct plane traffic.

Radio waves also carry the signals from your favorite radio stations, and your not-so-favorites. Radio waves may be the signal carriers, but it's you who make a radio work. The "Top 40" tunes, country, oldies, news programs, talk shows—you can pick them up on radios anywhere. You can pick them up at home, in your car or outside on the beach.

Radio Makes Waves

In 1922, 1.5 million radio receivers were in homes across the U.S. Five hundred fifty radio stations were in operation. In 1995, 500 million radios in the U.S. tuned in to one of 11,500 radio stations.

How many hours a day do you listen to your radio?

How can a car radio pick up your local station, even when you're miles away, going 55 mph? How do waves in the air that you can't hear or feel turn into music that you *can* hear *and* feel—if you play it loud enough?

In this book, you'll find out about the science—and the people—that make radio what it is. You'll discover surprising ways that radio affects your life. You'll get a first-hand look inside a radio station. You'll also get a peek behind the tuning knobs to find out what makes your radio tick.

Get ready, because we're on the air!

CHAPTER TWO

CATCH A RIDE ON THE AIRWAVES

What are **radio waves?** You can't see them, hear them, smell them, taste them or touch them, but they are everywhere!

Kinds Of Waves

You already know about water waves and how they move. You've probably also made waves of your own by flicking the ends of a jump rope. These are both **physical waves** (FIZ i kul WAYVZ). The **matter** (MAT ur) that makes up the water and the jump rope is moving in a wave pattern.

Radio waves are a kind of **electromagnetic wave** (ee lek troh mag NET ik WAYV). Electromagnetic waves are made up of moving **electrical fields** (ee LEK tri kul FEELDZ), or energy. They don't need matter to move. They can move through empty space at the speed of light, 186,282 miles per second! Some electromagnetic waves can travel not only through outer space, but also through air—and solid matter.

Waves are nature's way of moving energy from one place to another. For example, when we see a star at night, we are seeing light energy from that star. Carried by electromagnetic waves, the star's energy travels trillions of miles to reach our eyes. During a radio broadcast, the station transmits radio waves—a kind of electromagnetic wave—through the air. Those waves come through the walls of our homes to our radios.

Radio waves can travel through empty space, and through solid objects.
They come right through the walls of our homes to our radios.

The Parts Of A Wave

All electromagnetic waves—and physical waves—carry information. They tell us something about the waves. When you look at a water wave you can see how high it is—**amplitude** (AM pluh tood). You can see how fast it is moving—velocity or speed. You can see how far apart the waves are—**wavelength** (WAYV lenkth).

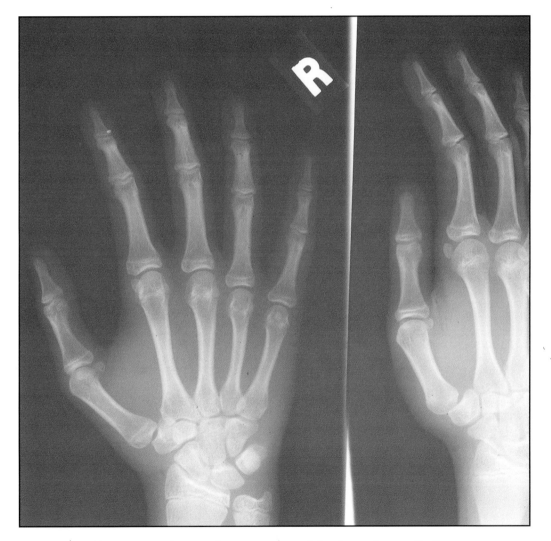

X-rays are electromagnetic rays that can move right through your body.

With special equipment, you can see the same things in an electromagnetic wave—amplitude, velocity and wavelength. If you know the velocity and wavelength of any kind of wave, you can figure out its **frequency** (FREE kwun see), or waves per second.

Frequency is important in radio waves. Using electricity, you can create radio waves with different frequencies. You measure frequency in **hertz** (HURTS). A radio wave with one frequency can carry a different message than a radio wave with another frequency. That's how you can choose from different radio stations.

Waves At Work

There are many different kinds of electromagnetic waves. Have you ever heard **static** (STAT ik) on the radio when a thunderstorm is nearby? That's electromagnetic waves made by lightning. Have you ever had an X-ray? Electromagnetic waves passed right through your body. They landed on film and made a picture of your bones.

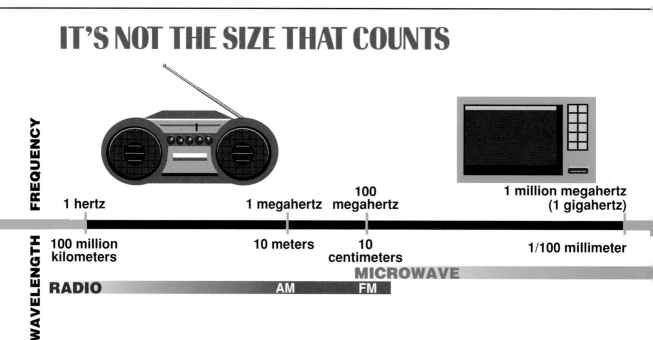

IT'S NOT THE SIZE THAT COUNTS

FREQUENCY

1 hertz	1 megahertz	100 megahertz	1 million megahertz (1 gigahertz)

WAVELENGTH

100 million kilometers	10 meters	10 centimeters	1/100 millimeter

MICROWAVE

RADIO   AM   FM

Radio waves are just one kind of electromagnetic wave. There are also microwaves, light rays and X-rays—and more—that operate at different frequencies. As you go from radio waves to X-rays, the waves get smaller and smaller and have more energy.

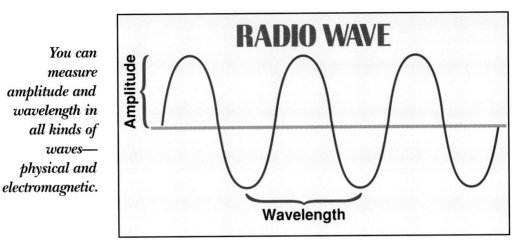

You can measure amplitude and wavelength in all kinds of waves—physical and electromagnetic.

When you slip a bag of popcorn into the microwave, the popcorn absorbs electromagnetic waves. In the popcorn, the waves change to heat. When you feel the sun warming your skin, you're feeling electromagnetic waves. In fact, whenever you look at anything you're seeing electromagnetic waves—light!

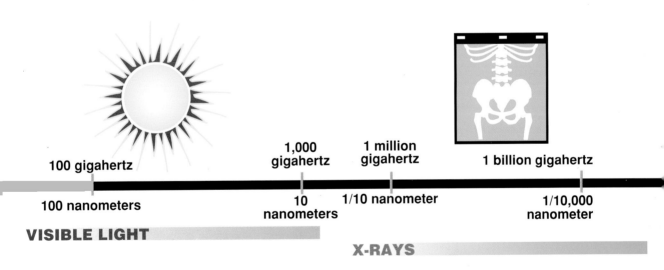

In fact, light rays and X-rays are so much smaller, that scientists measure them in nanometers (wavelengths) instead of hertz (frequency). It takes 1 million nanometers to make a millimeter.

CHAPTER THREE

GETTING THE SIGNAL

With all those **electromagnetic wave**s moving around in space, it's not very hard to believe that some would bump into your radio. Your radio doesn't react to every electromagnetic wave it comes across. It only recognizes **radio waves.** Then it turns them into voices and music. All you need is an **antenna** (an TEN uh), some **circuitry** (SUR kuh tree) and a little bit of electricity.

Traveling Piggyback

When you turn on your favorite radio station, you are tuned into its special **frequency.** In the radio station, the DJ speaks into a microphone that changes his or her words into **electrical signals** (ee LEK tri kul SIG nulz). Wires carry these electrical impulses to an **amplifier** (AM pluh fii ur). From the amplifier they go to the station's transmitter.

After the DJ's intro, the music starts. The DJ's CD (compact disk) player doesn't need a microphone. It sends the music—translated into electrical signals—straight to the amplifier. Again the last stop is the transmitter.

Transmitters are kept in boxes about the size of a home water heater. On the box's front panels, you might find all sorts of meters, knobs and switches. Transmitters put out a lot of heat. To keep them at the right temperature, there are blower fans at the base.

Small radio stations may have the transmitter right in the station. The transmitting tower is right outside. However, the transmitter does not have to be in the same building as the studio. A station's transmitter may be located many miles from the station.

At the radio station, your voice is turned into electrical signals by the microphone.

WHAT'S INSIDE?

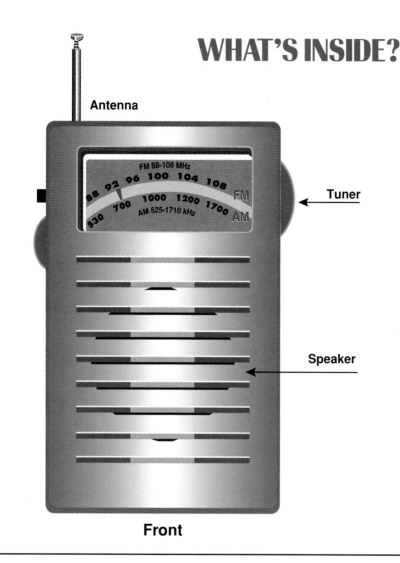

Antenna

FM 88-108 MHz

88 92 96 100 104 108

530 700 1000 1200 1700

AM 525-1710 kHz

FM

AM

Tuner

Speaker

Front

Transmitters away from the station are kept in a small building near the base of the transmitting tower. To get the radio signal from the station to the transmitter, the radio station sends a microwave signal. The microwave signal carries all the information to a microwave dish antenna at the transmitter.

At the transmitter, an **oscillator** (AH sil ay ter) makes a radio wave at a special frequency. The **Federal Communications Commission** (FED ur ul kuh myoo ni KAY shunz kuh MISH un) (FCC) assigns the frequency to the radio station.

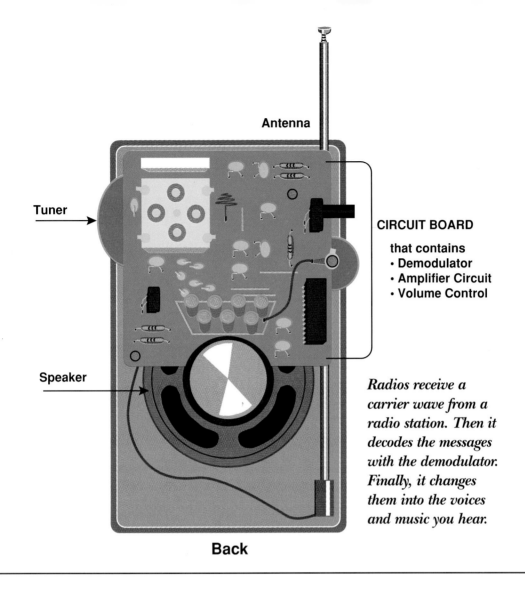

Antenna

Tuner →

CIRCUIT BOARD

that contains
• Demodulator
• Amplifier Circuit
• Volume Control

Speaker →

Radios receive a carrier wave from a radio station. Then it decodes the messages with the demodulator. Finally, it changes them into the voices and music you hear.

Back

The FCC was created in the 1920s. Back then all radio stations broadcast on one of two frequencies. Sometimes stations tried to work things out by agreeing to broadcast during different hours. Other stations tried to drown their competitors out by sending stronger signals.

The confusion was so bad that radio almost didn't survive. However in 1927, the government created the Federal Radio Commission (later called the FCC) to help sort things out. Now, each radio station is allowed to broadcast only on its own frequency.

13

The special frequency radio wave that the oscillator makes is called a **carrier wave** (KAYR ee ur WAYV). The DJ's audio, or voice, signals and the music signals combine with the carrier wave with the help of the transmitter's **modulator** (MAHJ uh lay tur). The sound signals get a piggyback ride on the strong carrier wave as they're broadcast.

Finally the modulated—combined or changed—radio wave gets amplified even more before being transmitted in all directions from the station's **antenna.**

Today radios come in all shapes and sizes. You might even be able to save enough to buy your own.

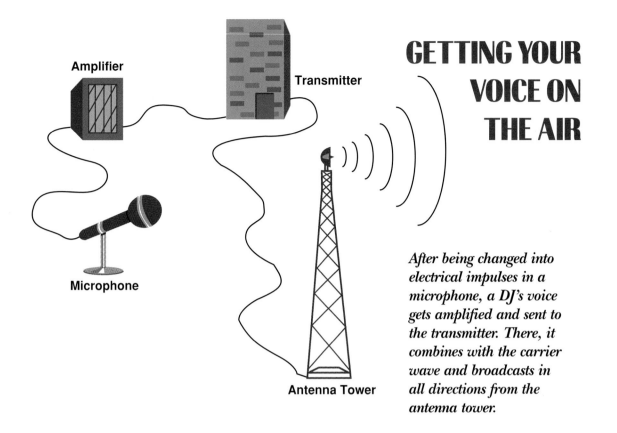

Amplifier

Transmitter

GETTING YOUR VOICE ON THE AIR

Microphone

Antenna Tower

After being changed into electrical impulses in a microphone, a DJ's voice gets amplified and sent to the transmitter. There, it combines with the carrier wave and broadcasts in all directions from the antenna tower.

Into Your Radio

Your radio's antenna picks up the carrier waves. Then it changes them into weak **electrical currents** (ee LEK tri kul KUR ents). The weak electrical currents are boosted by an **amplifier** circuit.

At the same time the **demodulator** (dee MAH joo layt ur), or detector, separates the **audio signal** (AW dee oh SIG nul)—voice and music—from the carrier wave. Then this **electrical signal,** carrying the audio part of the broadcast, gets amplified again. Finally, it goes to the speakers. The speakers change the electrical signals into the sounds you hear.

Your radio's antenna picks up all the radio waves from all the radio stations in range. To keep you from hearing 20 stations at once, your radio uses a **tuner** (TOON er). The tuner will only pick up the frequency you choose with the tuner control.

CHAPTER FOUR

UP AND DOWN THE DIAL

Almost every radio gives you a choice between AM and FM stations. What's the difference? It has to do with the kind of **carrier wave** the radio station uses. **Amplitude modulation** (AM pluh tood mahj uh LAY shun), or AM stations, modulate their carrier waves by changing the **amplitude,** or height, of the radio waves. **Frequency modulation** (FREE kwun see mahj uh LAY shun), or FM stations, modulate their carrier waves by changing the **frequency.**

Today most radios are AM/FM, with more radio stations on the FM band. When radios first came out, they were all AM. However, AM signals are easily blocked by any kind of electricity.

People listening to AM stations get **static** because of lightning, electrical appliances, fluorescent lights—and even spark plugs! Driving near high voltage lines on the highway can cause static on your car's AM radio. FM reception is much clearer than AM, and is almost static-free.

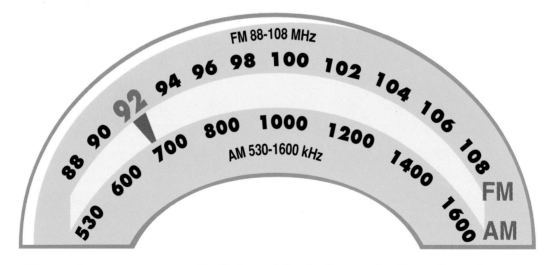

The numbers you see on a radio dial stand for the frequencies the radio stations are using. The station 92 FM broadcasts at 92 MHz.

AM frequencies range from about 530 kHz (kilohertz) to 1600 kHz. More powerful FM frequencies go from 88 MHz (megahertz) to 108 MHz. On a shortwave (SW) radio the SW frequency bands run from 6 MHz to 18 MHz. On the other end of the scale are frequencies used to transmit TV signals. Bands like VHF (very high frequency) and UHF (ultra high frequency) all have frequencies over 108 MHz.

Signals From Around The World

Have you ever tuned in to a radio station only to have it fade out again? While driving in a car, have you been able to keep one radio station you started with, but lose all the others?

The strength of a radio station's signal depends upon the height of the station's antenna and the power output of its transmitter. The higher the antenna, and the more powerful the transmitter, the further the radio waves can travel.

The World's First Real Radio Station

The first radio station ever to get a license from the U.S. government was KDKA in Pittsburgh, Pennsylvania. On November 2, 1920, KDKA made its first broadcast. They announced the results of the presidential election. Warren Harding had defeated James Cox.

That wasn't the only first for KDKA. They also broadcast the first sporting event— a boxing match—the first onstage theatrical performance and the first live radio church service.

The station's studio was in a small shack built on top of an eight-story building. Later, when they began to invite live performers, they added a tent to protect them from the weather.

However, the tent couldn't keep out the noise of the train that went by every now and then. During one show, a singer had to stop in the middle of a song because a moth flew into his mouth!

Soon the radio station moved indoors. Many others did the same. By 1922 there were 550 radio stations and 1.5 million listeners!

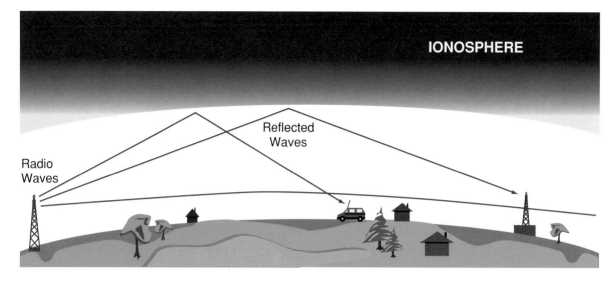

Radio waves travel in straight lines. So, they need help in order to go around the globe. Radio waves can bounce off the ionosphere high in the Earth's atmosphere, or be relayed by satellites in orbit.

Radio waves, like light waves, travel in a straight line. No matter how tall you build your antenna, sooner or later your radio waves are going to run into the ground. If they don't hit the ground, they'll go off into space.

Radio waves can't follow the curve of the Earth—without help. Radio waves angling up toward the sky can reflect off the Earth's **ionosphere** (ii AH nuh sfeer). They bounce back down to radio receivers on the ground. This way, you might be able to receive a radio station that's broadcasting from across the country!

This effect works especially well at night, when the sun's energy is blocked. Then the part of the ionosphere that reflects radio waves is higher. The radio waves can make longer bounces.

Did You Know Radio Waves Carry TV Signals?

If you're interested in TV try out another book in the YOU MAKE IT WORK series—TELEVISION.

Beginning Radio

In 1895, Guglielmo Marconi sent the first radio signals. Twenty-five years later, the first radio station, KDKA in Pittsburgh, Pennsylvania, began broadcasting. In the 1920s and '30s, radios were large and very expensive. Usually, there was only one radio in a home. Kids couldn't afford to buy one of their own. They surely wouldn't want to carry one outside on a walk.

However, kids did build their own simple radio sets—called crystal sets. The antenna for the crystal set was a long wire, stretched out from a kid's bedroom window. You had to connect the antenna to something high, like a tree, at least 50 feet away. The detector stage, like today's demodulator, was a mineral crystal—like galena—and a wire.

You got the crystal set to pick up the strongest signal with a coil of wire and a variable condenser, like today's tuner. The strongest radio stations were not very strong at all. The crystal set had no amplifier, so you had to use earphones to hear the radio.

Crystal sets were a great way to experiment with radio. They didn't cost much to build. Plus, they didn't need batteries or electricity to run. You can still buy kits for crystal sets today in some stores.

Crystal sets have the same parts as modern radios—a variable capacitor (black disk), an antenna (yellow wire) and a demodulator (the small part connected to two springs).

19

CHAPTER FIVE

INSIDE A RADIO STATION

What do you like to listen to on the radio? If you're like most people, it's music. However, the radio can also bring you live sports broadcasts, news programs and talk shows.

Do you remember that storm that might have cancelled school? While you were still in bed, the station manager, or program director, was getting together a list of cancelled activities. Schools, businesses and clubs called the information in. Then the station manager handed the list to the DJ. He or she read them over the air.

DJs don't just announce music and read the news. They also have to make sure the music and commercials play at the right times.

This kind of information is important to people in the community. By including community service spots like this, the station manager knows that more people will listen to the station.

Each radio station you find on the dial has its own kind of personality, or programming. Some play rock and roll. Some play country. Some broadcast mostly talk shows, and so on. It's up to the program director and the station manager to give the station its "personality."

The station manager organizes and manages the station, down to the smallest detail. The program director plans the programs the station should broadcast. Together they decide on the best programming for their station.

Station managers work closely with DJs, who play the music and commercials on the air. Inside the DJ's booth, or studio, you'll find a control board, tape machines, CD machines, microphones and music racks. The DJ operates the control board to turn his or her microphone on and off. The control board also helps to play the music and commercials in the right order.

Radio Rocks The World

1922 to 1952 was the golden age of radio. People depended on radio to bring them entertainment and news. However on October 30, 1938, they couldn't tell the difference. When Orson Welles read H.G. Wells's *The War of the Worlds,* he made the story sound so real that listeners panicked. They thought Martians had landed on Earth!

However, as computers become more powerful and less expensive, small- and medium-sized radio stations are getting computerized. The computer can handle all of the music, commercials and phone calls that a station needs in order to run. In these stations, all the DJ has to do is talk into the microphone and run the computer controls.

Almost all radio stations have someone working on news reports. At a small station, the news people may get their news from a newspaper, or from a national news source. A large radio station has reporters who go out and collect news stories. They also edit them and get them ready to broadcast. Some radio stations, especially larger ones, may have script writers or copywriters for commercials.

To make a talk show, the radio station sets up a studio with a table. The table has microphones built into it. They also use a multi-line phone and a *cough switch*. The cough switch lets the people using the microphone turn it off when they don't want to be heard.

When the mikes are turned on, the broadcast board operator takes control of the show. The operator adjusts the volume, plays commercials and screens phone calls.

The business of broadcasting a radio program is changing every day. Many programs come to the station over a **satellite** (SAT il iit), such as the national news or professional sports broadcasts. However, most times in-state sports events are still brought to you by networks of phone lines. More and more, whole programs—including music announcers and commercials—are recorded first, then sent by satellite.

Rockin' Around The Clock

In the early 1950s, radio listeners were starting to turn into TV watchers. Alan Freed, a DJ in Cleveland, Ohio, tried to lure young listeners back to the radio with rock and roll.

TOP TUNES THROUGHOUT THE YEARS

1955	Cherry Pink And Apple Blossom White	Perez "Prez" Prado
	Sincerely	The McGuire Sisters
	(We're Gonna) Rock Around The Clock	Bill Haley & His Comets
	Sixteen Tons	"Tennessee" Ernie Ford
	Love Is A Many-Splendoured Thing	Four Aces
	The Yellow Rose Of Texas	Mitch Miller
1965	(I Can't Get No) Satisfaction	The Rolling Stones
	Yesterday	The Beatles
	Mrs. Brown You've Got A Lovely Daughter	Herman's Hermits
	I Got You Babe	Sonny & Cher
	Help!	The Beatles
	Turn! Turn! Turn! (To Everything There Is A Season)	The Byrds
1975	Love Will Keep Us Together	The Captain & Tenille
	He Don't Love You (Like I Love You)	Tony Orlando & Dawn
	Bad Blood	Neil Sedaka
	Island Girl	Elton John
	Fly, Robin, Fly	Silver Connection
1985	Say You, Say Me	Lionel Richie
	We Are The World	USA for Africa
	Careless Whisper	Wham!
	Can't Fight This Feeling	REO Speedwagon
	Shout	Tears for Fears
	Money For Nothing	Dire Straits
1995	Gangsta's Paradise	Coolio
	Waterfalls	TLC
	Creep	TLC
	Kiss From A Rose	Seal
	On Bended Knee	Boyz II Men

When Radio Really Was Live

In the early days of radio, an audience came to watch radio shows performed. Directors directed actors and actresses who read their scripts in front of a microphone.

Radio stars often wore costumes and used a few props—like guns or purses. They had a live orchestra playing in the background.

Sound effects people used whatever they could think of to add the sound of knocking on doors, thunder and lightning, and horses running across the plains.

CHAPTER SIX

THE MANY WAYS WE USE ONE-WAY RADIO

What do remote control toys, beepers, endangered animals and astronauts have in common? They all use one-way radios, just like you use when you turn on your radio for some background music. Here are just a few ways that one-way radio helps us.

Remote Control Toys

All remote control toys come in two pieces—the transmitter and the receiver. The remote control you hold in your hand is the transmitter. It sends out different radio signals for each command you give. Turning the wheel to turn right is one signal. Pushing the lever to slow down is another.

Scientists use the information they gather from radios to learn about animals like this turtle in their natural habitats.

LOCATING WITH RADIO

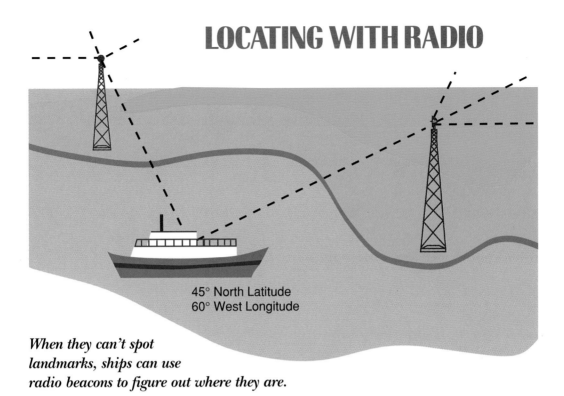

45° North Latitude
60° West Longitude

When they can't spot landmarks, ships can use radio beacons to figure out where they are.

The receiver in the remote control car, boat, or plane receives the signal and does what you tell it to do. Using one-way radio gives you an invisible hand to move your toy—no strings attached!

Beepers

Lots of people use **pagers** (PAYJ urz), or beepers. Doctors, delivery people, businesspeople, even some parents are a few. It might happen at home, or you might have seen it on TV. The beeper goes off, and the person goes to the phone to check what the message might be. If you need to stay in touch, a beeper can reach you just about anywhere.

However, if radio signals are everywhere, how does the beeper know when *not* to beep? Each beeper is made to beep only at a certain **frequency.** This way when a businessperson gets paged, the frequency of the radio signal does not affect the doctor sitting next to her.

Radios In The Wild

One way scientists can get first-hand information about animals in the wild is to use radio collars. Scientists can't follow a wild wolf pack everywhere it goes. So, they capture one wolf, put on a radio collar, and let it loose again. Then they follow the radio collar's signals using airplanes, helicopters or other vehicles.

Each radio collar broadcasts its own frequency. This way scientists know exactly which animal they are tracking. They can learn about animal habits, habitats and how long animals live—all without disturbing the animals too much.

Radio Points The Way

One-way radios also help in navigation, or finding the right direction. Radio beams help airplanes keep pilots on course, even when they can't see where they're going. Ships at sea use radio beacons to pinpoint their location. Radar, another kind of one-way radio, tracks airplanes and ships and helps direct traffic. Even astronauts use radio signals to guide their spacecrafts!

Radio Fire Fighters

Scientists also use one-way transmitters as fire detectors. They drop the radios in hard-to-reach places, like mountainsides. If the radio detects a fire it sends a signal. Fire fighters pick up the signal on airplanes that fly over the area. With the help of the one-way radio, fire fighters can get to the scene of the fire quickly.

CHAPTER SEVEN

TALK RADIO

Radio can be more than just one-way—they talk and you listen. A lot of radio is two-way communication—they talk and you talk back!

CBs And Walkie-Talkies

One kind of two-way radio you probably know about is CB, or **citizens band** (SIT uh zunz BAND) radio. The **FCC** has set aside some radio frequencies for the use of businesses, and for people like you and your family.

Two-way radios are very important in emergencies. They get the call for help out fast.

Most CB radio is mobile, or moving, radio. People who have CB units in their cars or trucks can use them to talk to other people on the road who have CB units. If you listen to the talk on CBs, you'll hear about the weather, road conditions and emergency situations. Sometimes all you'll hear is gossip.

The range of a mobile CB unit is not more than a few miles. However, base stations can help CB signals go farther. A base station is a **transceiver** (tran SEE vur) that stays in one place all the time—like a home or business.

CB users often give themselves fun names, or *handles,* to use on the air. They also use a short-hand way of talking, called the **ten-code** (TEN kohd). "10-4" means that the message has been received and understood. At first police officers were the only people who used the ten-code. Now almost everyone on the CB does.

CB transmitters and receivers work exactly the same as one-way radios. However, with a CB, everyone has a transmitter *and* a receiver in one package. They can receive *and* send messages.

Public safety workers like police officers, fire fighters and emergency medical teams use a two-way radio very much like a CB. However, the frequencies they use are different than CBs. The U.S. armed forces also use two-way radios out in the field. They combine mobile radios, walkie-talkies and base stations.

Ham Radio

CBs and walkie-talkies, even with base station boosters, can only be picked up for a few miles. **Ham** (HAM) radio, or amateur radio, can reach to the other side of the world!

Every ham operator has to pass a test given by the FCC. The test asks questions about radio science and technology, and FCC rules. Morse code used to be very important to ham operators. Now you can get a ham operator's license without knowing code.

The Wave Of The Future—Satellite Sound And Visual Radio

Digital audio broadcast (DAB) gives listeners around the world great sound. It's free from static because it's broadcast from satellites! In 1992 cost kept many people from using DAB. The special tuner needed to change satellite signals into sound cost over $2,000.

Less expensive technology, made possible with computers, is visual radio. No, it's not television. However, sounds and printed words are sent through the airwaves. Push a button and the radio will show you the title of the song you're hearing. Push it again and you can get information about the weather!

Amateur radio is true international radio. By using the **ionosphere** to reflect their **radio waves,** ham operators bounce their radio signals around the world (see page 18). However, you can't always depend on the ionosphere. Solar activity can keep it from reflecting radio waves very well.

Amateurs have their own communications **satellites,** called the Oscar satellites. Only ham operators are allowed to use Oscar satellites.

Amateurs all over the world work together in emergencies. During floods, earthquakes, hurricanes and other disasters, sometimes all communications—phones, TV and others—may fail. Ham operators get the word out. Sometimes ham operators are the only way the rest of the world knows that there is an emergency.

amplifier (AM pluh fii ur) - the part of a radio circuit that increases the strength of a signal

amplitude (AM pluh tood) - distance from the baseline of a wave to its crest, the height of a wave; in sound, amplitude determines volume or loudness

amplitude modulation (AM) (AM pluh tood mahj uh LAY shun) - in radio transmission, the amplitude of the carrier wave is changed in relationship to the audio signal; in radio reception, the band on the receiver between 530 kHz and 1600 kHz

antenna (an TEN uh) - wire or other metal object that transmits—sends out—and receives—picks up—radio waves

audio signal (AW dee oh SIG nul) - the part of a radio wave broadcast by a radio station that carries sound information

carrier wave (KAYR ee ur WAYV) - radio wave sent out by a radio station at a special frequency that carries the audio signal

circuitry (SUR kuh tree) - all the electrical parts that make up an electrical device, like a radio

citizens band (CB) (SIT uh zunz BAND) - two-way radio communications; the FCC reserves special frequencies for people and businesses to use

demodulator (dee MAH joo layt ur) - the part of a radio receiver that separates the audio signal from the carrier wave

electrical current (ee LEK tri kul KUR ent) - flow of electrons along a conductor—like a wire (like **electrical signals**—ee LEK tri kul SIG nulz)

electrical field (ee LEK tri kul FEELD) - an area, or space, where there is an electrical effect, or force

electromagnetic waves (ee lek tro mag NET ik WAYVZ) - waves made up of both electrical and magnetic fields—X-rays, ultraviolet rays, visible light rays, radio waves, etc.

Federal Communications Commission (FCC) (FED ur ul kuh myoo ni KAY shunz kuh MISH un) - a U.S. government agency that regulates radio wave and wire communications; it assigns frequencies and grants licenses to radio and television stations

frequency (FREE kwun see) - the number of waves (or cycles, or vibrations) per second, measured in hertz (Hz); 1,000 Hz = 1 kilohertz (kHz), 1 million Hz = 1 megahertz (MHz)

frequency modulation (FM) (FREE kwun see mahj uh LAY shun) - in radio transmission, the frequency of the carrier wave is changed in relationship to the audio signal; in radio reception, the band on the receiver between 88 MHz and 108 MHz

ham (HAM) - licensed amateur radio operator

hertz (Hz) (HURTS) - how frequency is measured; the number of waves (or vibrations or cycles) per second

ionosphere (ii AH nuh sfeer) - the part of the Earth's atmosphere between 50 and 250 miles above the surface; radio waves can be reflected off it and go around the whole world

matter (MAT ur) - what everything is made of

modulator (MAHJ uh lay tur) - the part of a radio transmitter that changes the carrier wave to carry the audio signal

oscillator (AH sil ay ter) - a device in a radio transmitter that makes carrier waves

pager (PAYJ ur) - one-way radio that alerts the person who carries it to get in touch with someone else, usually by telephone

physical wave (FIZ i kul WAYV) - wave that needs matter to travel through, like a water wave

radio waves (RAY dee oh WAYVZ) - invisible waves that can carry information through the air or empty space at the speed of light

satellite (SAT il iit) - an object that circles the Earth above the atmosphere; it can receive and transmit radio waves

static (STAT ik) - hissing, crackling or other noises made in radio receivers by electricity

ten-code (TEN kohd) - short-hand way of communication used on CB radios

transceiver (tran SEE vur) - a radio unit that can both transmit and receive, like a CB radio or ham radio

tuner (TOON er) - the part of a radio receiver that finds a specific radio frequency or station

wavelength (WAYV lenkth) - the distance between two crests, or two other parts that are the same, of a wave

INDEX